T0198771

YOU ARE A GIFT FROM THE STARS... BORN TO LIGHT UP THE WORLD

Written and illustrated by

Kristina Elliot

Balboa Press books may be ordered through booksellers or by contacting:

Balboa Press
A Division of Hay House
1663 Liberty Drive
Bloomington, IN 47403
www.balboapress.com
844-682-1282

Interior Image Credit: Kristina Elliot

ISBN: 979-8-7652-3587-4 (sc)
ISBN: 979-8-7652-3588-1 (hc)
ISBN: 979-8-7652-3589-8 (e)

Print information available on the last page.

Balboa Press rev. date: 11/17/2022

BALBOA.PRESS
A DIVISION OF HAY HOUSE

I would like to dedicate this book to all the lightworkers, Starseeds, extraterrestrials and spiritual teachers who have helped awaken me to a whole new reality, in which we are all brothers and sisters in a vast galactic community.

Do you ever feel like you don't fit in?

Like you're a fish out of water?

Or a spotted zebra in a herd of stripes?

Are you just a bit too smart?

Or a little too nerdy?

Do other kids call you names that make you feel angry or sad?

Do you sometimes act out, because you don't feel comfortable in your own skin?

Like you're missing something that makes you like everyone else?

If you've ever wondered why you feel so out of place...

There might be a simple answer.

Maybe you're a STARSEED.

"A STARSEED?" you might be wondering. "I've never heard of that."

You're not alone. Lots of people don't know about STARSEEDS. But more people are learning about them every day.

Like the name implies, STARSEEDS are humans who have lived other lives in distant star systems.

In fact, this might be your first life on the Earth. Which would explain why it feels a little weird.

Wait…you didn't think Earth was the only place in the universe where life exists, did you?

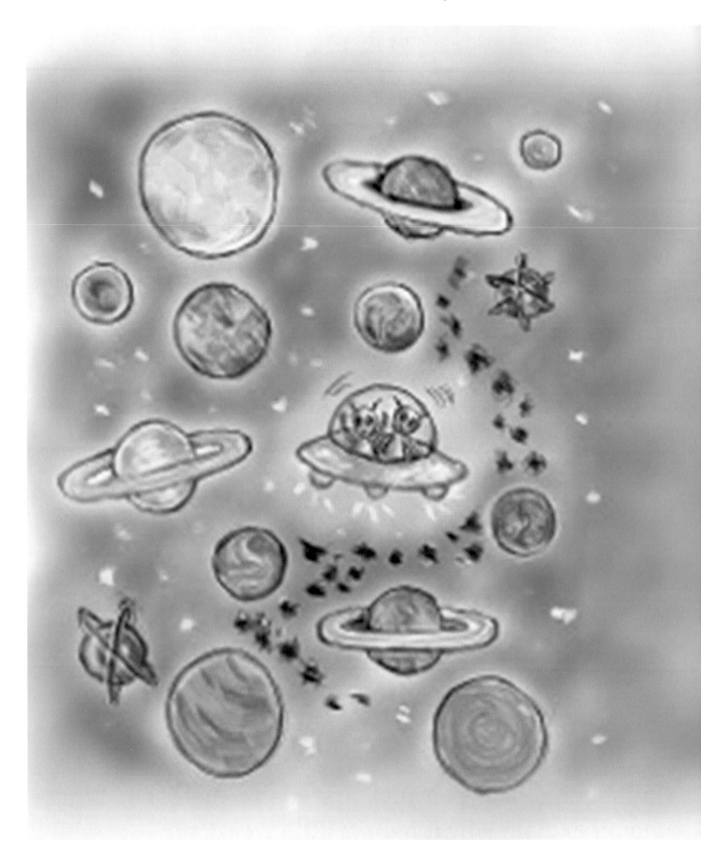

Based on reliable sources, there may be billions of inhabited planets—many more advanced than we are.

What might these Star beings look like? Well, some of them might be very much like us, but others might look quite different.

But here's the really interesting thing...although our bodies may look different, deep inside we all have something that's very much the same.

It's more powerful than the brain, and it lives forever. It's what makes us unique and connects us to everything in the universe.

You may have heard of it. It's called the **SOUL.**

Now just imagine that in another life you lived in a different kind of body and had very different skills.

Maybe your planet was highly evolved and, thanks to your **SOUL,** you stopped having wars and learned to live together in peace.

And maybe, just maybe, your special skills were needed here on Earth, so we could learn to be the kind of people it needed us to become.

People who wouldn't keep acting like jerks by killing each other and destroying the planet.

You see the Earth is in dire need of a makeover. We haven't been doing such a good job taking care of it—or each other.

And that means we have to make some big changes in the way we think and act.

So when the call went out in the Universe, your **SOUL** was brave enough to volunteer for the mission.

Now here you are. The only problem is—you don't remember any of this.

You just feel like a human being wearing the wrong skin suit.

So you sit in your room, stare out at the stars, and cry...

"What on Earth am I doing here?!

But don't despair.

You're actually in very good
company. Because there are
millions of STARSEEDS on the
Earth right now.

You're NOT alone.

Just like you, they were brave
enough to answer the call to
help our Earth become the best
it can be.

How do you know you're a STARSEED?

Maybe you're really interested in science.

Or you may feel a strong connection to animals.

Maybe you just know things...sometimes even before they happen.

Chances are you're always looking
at the sky...especially at night

Most of all…you find yourself yearning for a place you can't even remember.

But even though you might feel a little lost, being a STARSEED could mean **you're destined to do great things!**

You see, STARSEEDS have been on the Earth for hundreds—even thousands—of years.

They might have been born as...

Native American warriors

Egyptian queens

Even World War I pilots

And even though they might have grown up feeling alone, it helped them focus on making the most of their special talents.

Because STARSEEDS are here to make the world a better place; with their talents, their words or just their determination.

Greta Thunberg, Abraham Lincoln, and Malala Yousafzai are great examples of heroic people who might have been born STARSEEDS

Greta Thunberg,
the young climate change activist, dedicated her life to saving the Earth.

Abe Lincoln,
our 16th president, helped free the slaves in America.

Malala Yousafzai
won the Nobel Peace Prize and risked her life to support education for girls in the Middle East.

Often STARSEEDS are born with special gifts to share with humanity. This may be in fields like music, science, literature, or sports.

Celebrities like **Elon Musk, Amanda Gorman and Bruno Mars** are probably STARSEEDS.

Elon Musk
is the co-founder of Tesla electric cars and SpaceX rocket ships.

Amanda Gorman
is one of America's most talented young poets.

Bruno Mars
is a popular singer, songwriter and record producer.

So you see, STARSEEDS are members of a very important club. They are the heroes who will help us to heal our planet—and ourselves.

So even if you feel like a misfit who doesn't belong here…you might be just what this planet needs.

You and millions of spazzes, nerds, weirdos and other wonderfully unique humans are here for a very important reason.

You just have to figure out what it is.

So go find your tribe my friend. And the next time you feel alone remember—the whole Universe is cheering you on.

Your galactic family is watching, and they know you will make the world a better place—just by being YOU.

Printed in the United States
by Baker & Taylor Publisher Services